YUKON·RIVER

YUKON·RIVER

An Adventure to the Gold Fields of the Klondike

Written and photographed by Peter Lourie

Boyds Mills Press

PROSPECTOR & COMPANION

To my mother and father

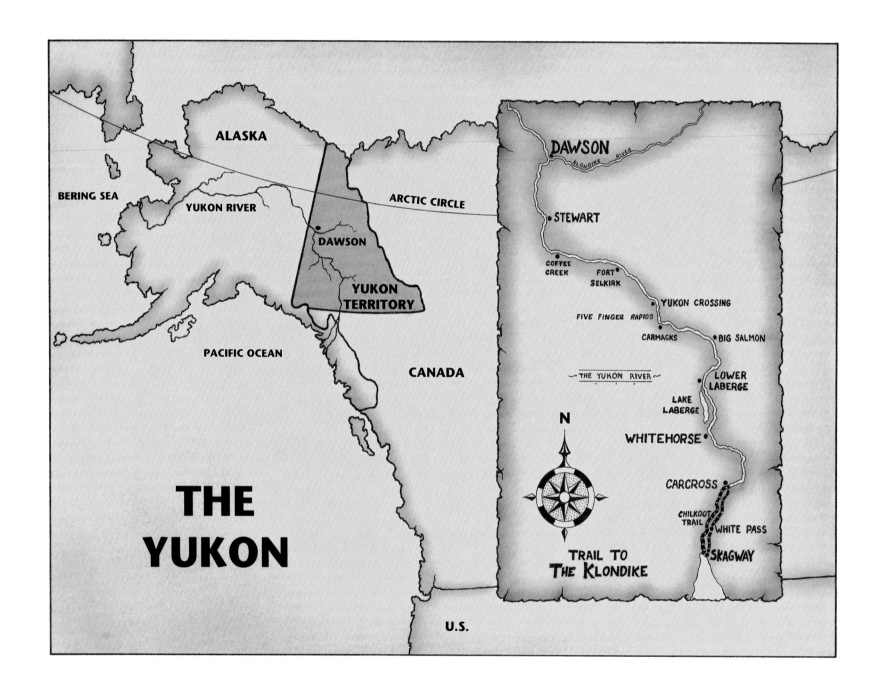

THE YUKON

ALASKA

BERING SEA

YUKON RIVER

ARCTIC CIRCLE

DAWSON

YUKON TERRITORY

PACIFIC OCEAN

CANADA

U.S.

DAWSON

KLONDIKE RIVER

STEWART

COFFEE CREEK

FORT SELKIRK

YUKON CROSSING

FIVE FINGER RAPIDS

CARMACKS

BIG SALMON

THE YUKON RIVER

LOWER LABERGE

LAKE LABERGE

WHITEHORSE

N

CARCROSS

CHILKOOT TRAIL

WHITE PASS

SKAGWAY

TRAIL TO THE KLONDIKE

CONTENTS

Preface

There's a land where the mountains are nameless,
  And the rivers all run God knows where;
There are lives that are erring and aimless,
  And deaths that just hang by a hair;
There are hardships that nobody reckons;
  There are valleys unpeopled and still;
There's a land—oh, it beckons and beckons,
  And I want to go back—and I will.

Robert W. Service

Northern lights in the Yukon

Though Europeans arrived in the region of the upper Yukon River in the 1840s, it was the gold rush of 1897–1899 that made Canada's Yukon famous. When gold nuggets were found in Bonanza Creek, which feeds the Klondike River, more than 100,000 people left their offices and farms and families. From all over the world people stricken with gold fever rushed to the Klondike region of the Yukon to claim their fortune. Of the 30,000 or so who reached Dawson, only a few hundred struck it rich.

Ever since I was a boy, I'd dreamed of the Yukon. I'd yearned to follow the fourth-largest river in North America, the main route to the Klondike gold fields. The Yukon wilderness beckoned me just as it had once beckoned those thousands searching for gold, who came in such droves they were called "stampeders."

With the dream of striking it rich, the stampeders traveled a torturous 565 miles from Alaska's coast to the interior boomtown of Dawson near the Arctic Circle. I planned to follow that same golden trail. But in this age of automobiles and computers and overcrowded malls and cities, I was seeking something other than the precious metal, something rarer. I wanted to see the untamed wilderness. When I set out for the Yukon with my friend Ernie LaPrairie, I hoped to find a place the modern age had not yet spoiled.

The Chilkoot Trail and prospectors as far as the eye can see

Panning for gold

To Whitehorse

The Chilkoot Trail and the White Pass

Ernie and I began our trip by driving from the coast of Alaska over the White Pass. At the time of the gold rush, this was one of the two fastest routes to the Klondike. The other was the Chilkoot Trail. Both routes took the stampeders over the rugged, misty coastal mountains. The Northwest Mounted Police required each gold miner to take one ton of equipment and food along in order to survive the long journey. The problem was getting all that gear up and over the mountains and down the river to Dawson.

Jack London, author of *The Call of the Wild* and *White Fang*, was among those who stampeded north to the Klondike. He described the grueling trek over the White Pass this way:

"The horses died like mosquitoes in the first frost...They fell off the trail, what there was of it, and they went through it; in the river they drowned under their loads and were smashed to pieces against the boulders...."

Such horrible conditions forced many stampeders to give up and turn back.

Stampeders had to climb these misty mountains

To Laberge

Whitehorse

After driving over the White Pass, Ernie and I began our canoe trip from Whitehorse, the capital of the Yukon Territory. We were facing 460 miles of paddling between Whitehorse and Dawson.

Just above Whitehorse is the site of the once-famous Whitehorse Rapids, so named because the swirling whitewater resembled the manes of white horses. At one time the whole upper Yukon funneled into Miles Canyon and over these rapids, creating one of the greatest obstacles for the stampeders heading for the Klondike. The Whitehorse Rapids no longer exist, however. Recently a power dam was constructed on the river just above the city, and now the dangerous rocks lie deep underwater.

Whitehorse was a resting place for the stampeders who made it through the rapids. Today, 20,000 of the Yukon Territory's 29,000 residents now live in this modern city. It is easy to imagine how sparsely populated the rest of this wild territory, which is twice the size of the state of Oregon, must be.

Miles Canyon

Stampeders shooting Whitehorse Rapids

Ernie and I about to tackle the river

Before we left, we reported our trip to the Royal Canadian Mounted Police in case we ran into trouble. Then we stood by the fast river and plotted our course. There was only a hint of sunlight in one part of the sky. Winter seemed to be coming in fast, and we were eager to get going.

We hopped into our heavily loaded canoe, I in the bow and Ernie in the stern. We pushed out into the powerful eight-mile-per-hour current, and it swung the canoe around with a fierce jerk. The water was cold and clear but not entirely safe to drink. The Mounties had warned us to boil our drinking water or run the risk of getting a severe illness called "Beaver Fever."

We found that September was a good month to travel the Yukon River by canoe. The tourists had gone home, and mosquito season was over. We knew we had to be prepared for some cold-weather camping, though. The temperature would drop into the thirties at night and rise in the day to only 50° or 60°F. Soon the ice would make the river almost impossible to travel by boat.

A Fishing Camp

Ernie and I pulled over at a native fishing camp and found long poles that had been set up as fish racks for drying salmon fillets. The salmon run was over, and no one was around. The log cabins, their roofs packed with earth and moss, were old and sturdy. We went in one of the cabins, and I was struck by the idea that we could stay there all winter long if we wanted to. No one would bother us. I could almost smell salmon cooking on the old stove.

Salmon is dried and preserved on racks like this one

17

Salmon Run

The king (chinook) salmon makes one of the longest spawning runs of any fish in the world. From the middle of July to the end of August, she leaves the Bering Sea and starts up the Yukon, to spawn thousands of miles upriver. She eats nothing on her way, yet she averages about fifty miles a day against the swift current, passing all kinds of dangers, such as nets, logjams, and bears. At last she arrives at the very stream in which she herself was born. How she finds her way back to this spot is one of the wonders of nature. Some say she recognizes her birthplace by smell. Perhaps it is a chemical recognition, a kind of memory. Nevertheless, if she survives the hazards in the river, she will always reach her birthplace to spawn.

A Yukon fisherman of old and his prize catch

Lake Laberge

At the entrance to moody Lake Laberge, Ernie and I found the remnants of the old pilings that were built to stop the silt from drifting into the main channel and fouling the paddles of the riverboats, or paddlewheelers, as they were often called. The paddlewheelers kept the river alive with transportation and commerce, but the river was a challenge even to these big boats. It might take three days to run the 460 miles from Whitehorse to Dawson, but it would take some paddlewheelers five days to fight the swift current on their return trip. And after the October freeze, they could not run until late spring.

The wide, thirty-mile-long lake is unpredictable and extremely dangerous. If you're a boater, you don't want to be caught in the middle of the lake when a storm sweeps in. Within minutes, the lake can change from quiet water to a maelstrom of waves and rollers going every which way. Ernie and I found out for ourselves. We were hugging the east shore, and suddenly our canoe nearly swamped in some long rollers that came up on us fast. The waves came in from behind and to the side of the canoe, making it dangerous paddling. It was only our second day out, and we did not want to fall into the freezing water.

19

We camped on a pebbled beach

Most lakes calm down in the evening, but not Laberge. At night the wind seemed to kick up more than ever, so we thought it wise to make camp early. The night we stayed there, we found a great place on a pebbled beach to pitch our tent. A bald eagle in the very tip of the spruce behind us watched as we collected driftwood to start a fire. We cooked our meal away from where we set up our tent. This was standard bear precaution, for we were in grizzly country.

Because salmon season had just ended, we knew it was unlikely that we'd see bears looking for fish by the riverside. But bears do have an acute sense of smell, and they like to investigate new food sources, so we planned to keep our cooking gear and our food well away from our sleeping area. Another thing I decided was never to wipe my food-dirty or fish-greasy hands on the clothes I'd sleep in at night.

OFFICERS OF B DIVISION N.W.M.P. DAWSON

Lower Laberge

After the discovery of gold, travel boomed on the Yukon. Stampeders built trading posts and winter quarters. They explored side streams and panned the sandbars. The region was patrolled by the Northwest Mounted Police, the forerunners of today's Royal Canadian Mounted Police. Posts were built at most of the major tributaries of the Yukon River from Whitehorse to Dawson. There were fewer than 300 "Mounties" in the whole territory during the gold rush, but collectively they traveled more than 64,000 miles by dog team in the winter of 1898–1899 alone.

Ernie and I saw a Northwest Mounted Police post in mint condition at the abandoned village of Lower Laberge. The post was in such good shape that it was hard to believe it had been erected in 1897. Lower Laberge was where the stampeders had rested after their tiring lake crossing. During the time that the village was thriving, there were twenty buildings there. It survived as a woodcamp until 1953, supplying logs to fuel the paddlewheelers.

To Shipyard Island

Thirty-Mile

We left Laberge early in the morning to rejoin the rushing waters of the Yukon. Somewhere in the mist, coyotes howled. It was an eerie sound. The river hurried us twenty-five miles by lunchtime. The mist cleared, and we found a stark autumn wilderness on the Thirty-Mile section of the upper Yukon.

Misty Thirty-Mile

And after the mist cleared

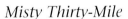

23

The paddlewheeler Casca

Shipyard Island

Shipyard Island was in a good location to service steamers coming out of the Thirty-Mile. Paddlewheelers, like the *Casca*, could find mooring there for the long winters. A vessel was slowly drawn up greased wooden skidways by cables wrapped around its hull. Horses slowly turned four capstans, winding up the cables and pulling the ship into place. It was then leveled and blocked up for winter storage.

Ernie and I stood among the ruins of the old ships while the lonely wind raked the tops of the spruce trees. We wondered why anyone would have invested in a paddlewheeler, since so many steamers were ruined on the rocks and sandbars of the upper Yukon.

To Five Finger Rapids

Big Salmon

To visit the old Northwest Mounted Police post and telegraph station on the Big Salmon River, we had to ferry across the fast water with the nose of our canoe pointed upstream, both of us paddling like crazy. Behind the telegraph post we found a small wooden structure in which the sled dogs had been housed.

We were tired and chose to sleep just below Big Salmon village on the sandbar of a big island. I pulled out the stove and made coffee in the cold dusk. While I cooked, Ernie scouted the area for grizzly. He found coyote and moose tracks but no evidence of bear, which made me feel better.

Instead of using our tent, we just pulled our canoe onto the beach and turned it over to use as a windbreak. We drew the tarp over the canoe belly and moored it out in front with a couple of heavy rocks. After the sun finally sank below the horizon, we ducked under the tarp and in no time were asleep.

Carmacks & Five Finger Rapids

After a night camping at Carmacks, a small town along the Klondike Highway, we paddled to Five Finger Rapids. We could hear the roar of rushing water ahead. Then we saw them—the rapids. Perhaps the best-known landmark on the upper Yukon River, Five Finger Rapids is exactly what the name suggests—five huge chunks of stone that look like cliffs in the middle of the river, with dangerous whitewater channels between the "fingers." Some canoeists had lost their lives there a few years back, and we'd been told over and over that we must stay to the right and paddle hard. But when we pulled into shore and climbed the nearby hill to take a better look, the waves in all of the channels, including the one on the right, seemed monstrous.

Five Finger Rapids

Paddlewheelers steamed through the rapids

We secured our gear and covered the whole canoe with a spray skirt so we'd ship less water in the cresting waves. The real danger to an open canoe in rapids is taking on too much water. A canoe will swamp easily when it becomes heavy and uncontrollable. We planned to paddle hard and keep the canoe straight on.

Inside the channel we plowed into the big waves. The bow came up so high in one wave that I couldn't reach the water with my paddle. Then we came crashing down into the water and the spray soaked me. We made it through, wet but safe.

29

To Fort Selkirk

Yukon Crossing

Winter travel from Whitehorse to Dawson initially followed the Yukon River ice. In 1902, after the traditional dogsleds were replaced by horses, a stage road was built, shortening the distance between the two towns by seventy-two miles. The road crossed the river at Yukon Crossing. Someone traveling the road during spring ice break-up or during the fall freeze might be stranded there for weeks, waiting for the river ice to be strong enough to run a stage over it.

One night we found Yukon Crossing. We pitched our tent in a willow grove near an old barn and roadhouse that used to be a stagecoach stop. The place was beautiful but lonely.

The roadhouse was in ruins

Prospectors searched for the big strike in creeks like Wolverine

Wolverine Creek

As we moved closer to Dawson and the Klondike, there seemed to be more creeks feeding into the Yukon. All of these creeks have been scoured by miners. We paddled up one called Wolverine Creek, which flowed swiftly out of the mountains, and pulled over to explore an abandoned mining camp. We found old boats rotting in the woods. We also found a stream that miners had redirected in order to run the water and gravel through sluice boxes, which are something like strainers. Some say that this method of mining is not good for the salmon, because spawning salmon will not return to a creek that has been tampered with. Miners see it differently, though. They must make their living, and they work hard to do it. To them, mining is not just striking it rich, it is years of backbreaking work to collect enough ounces of gold to survive.

Fort Selkirk

After paddling fifty miles in five hours, Ernie and I decided to camp early at Fort Selkirk, which was the first non-native settlement on the upper Yukon. Established first in 1848 by Robert Campbell, a fur trader for the Hudson Bay Company, Fort Selkirk was occupied on and off until 1952, when the Klondike Highway drew its 200 residents to nearby Pelly Crossing. Now the fort is like a museum that no one visits. Sitting on a high bluff with a sweeping vista of the surrounding mountains, Fort Selkirk is preserved in perfect condition.

Selkirk on the Yukon

Mr. Roberts guided us through the school at the fort

In the little schoolhouse on the bluff overlooking the wide river, the caretaker of the fort, Danny Roberts, told me that the settlement had been left exactly as it was in the busy days of the paddlewheelers.

Mr. Roberts still lives much of the year in Fort Selkirk. He is a member of the Tutchone tribe, one of the Athapaskan groups. He told me his father used to come into the classroom and tell him they had to go hunting. He said he'd just get up from his desk and walk out of school and head off into the bush to hunt.

Mr. Roberts also explained that his tribal law prohibited overhunting, as well as killing a cow moose when it was with its calf. And calves could be killed only when a person was desperate for food. Another Tutchone law forbade killing a bear by the river. It was believed that the blood would flow in the water, and when the salmon ran again, there would be no catching fish in that spot.

Hunting was very important to the Tutchones. They needed food to carry them through the harsh winters. Even today, Mr. Roberts told us, the temperature plummets to 73° below zero for weeks at a time in the winter, and he cannot leave the fort.

*The Yukon in the glow
of the northern lights*

Fort Selkirk was one of the most beautiful places to camp along the river. I walked through the deserted Mountie post, the school, the old trading offices, and the barns and got a rich sense of the past.

After dinner, a meal of arctic grayling that I caught below the bluff, Ernie read a copy of Robert Service's *Spell of the Yukon* with a flashlight while I stood beneath the frigid sky until the northern lights turned it green in all kinds of shifting shapes. Somewhere in the darkness, I heard the call of geese heading south for the winter. I felt the chill of the arctic wind and thought of home.

35

To Dawson

Coffee Creek

Our next camp was on an island across from Coffee Creek, named so by miners because of the color of the water.

After a peaceful night, we awoke to a heavy mist. The wind must have been coming straight off the polar ice cap, because it chilled us to the bone. We pushed off into the thick morning fog. There was something spooky about paddling in a river with so many islands and not knowing exactly which shoreline was island and which was mainland.

The day began with thick fog and icy winds

As the morning wore on, the fog gradually lifted, and the day became sunny and cool, with no fog in sight. We passed the White River. This is one place where silt from the glaciers to the west enters the Yukon. We could actually hear millions of pieces hitting our canoe. The sound was like the steady hiss of air being released from a tire.

Though it had been many days of hard paddling, we decided to continue into the night. About 10:30 P.M. the darkness finally swallowed the light. The days were getting shorter. We followed the North Star, and then the northern lights began to shift against the sky. We smelled woodsmoke in the air. It might have been a campfire, but more likely it was the smell of a recent forest fire.

We knew we were heading in the right direction, because we were not fighting any current. We were moving a swift ten miles an hour in the dark. Islands were ghostly shapes looming in the river night. At this rate, we would reach Dawson by morning.

Reindeer Creek

We ran aground on a sandbar in the dark and had to pole off it with our paddles. Around midnight, after eighty-two miles of paddling in one day, we found an island—or it found us. We ran into it. We threw all our gear down on the ground, pulled the canoe up, and flopped down into our sleeping bags with the tarp over us to keep off the heavy dew of the northern night. The temperature would drop below freezing.

When we woke and rubbed the sleep from our eyes, we found that the dew had soaked our bags, but we took comfort from the fact that we'd spend that night in a hotel in Dawson. I checked the map and discovered we had camped on an island just opposite Reindeer Creek.

Where were we?
We found out in the morning

Dawson today and yesterday, when stampeders would turn out for a big race down a Dawson street

Dawson at Last

We often let the canoe drift as we neared Dawson, because we didn't want to hurry. As soon as the river trip was over, we'd be heading back to our jobs, and this magnificent wilderness would become a memory.

We heard the town of Dawson before we saw it. The sound of civilization made my stomach queasy after so many days of silence. But we had made it. We had reached the end of our journey down the Yukon River.

For the stampeders, Dawson was the beginning of a quest for gold in the Klondike. But most of the stampeders never became miners. Many who reached Dawson discovered that almost all the gold-bearing ground was staked. They returned south. And Dawson presented hardships for those who remained; in fact, it was so overcrowded that one winter a famine broke out.

41

BARTLETT BROS. PACK TRAIN DAWSON 1899

Bonanza Creek

The Discovery on Bonanza Creek in the Klondike

It was George Washington Carmack, along with two friends, who in 1896 made the discovery that changed the Yukon for all time. The story goes that he had a dream about two king salmon with gold nuggets for armor and twenty-dollar gold coins for eyes. He took this as a sign to go fishing where the Klondike River meets the Yukon. Two of his native friends, Skookum Jim and Tagish Charlie, met him there, but the fishing was no good. They poled up the Klondike River to the Bonanza Creek. One of the men put his hand in the river and pulled up a gold nugget the size of his thumb. Later Carmack would say the gold lay in the creekbed as thick as cheese on a sandwich.

News of the gold strike traveled fast.

The Klondike flows into the Yukon at Dawson

These prospectors are packed and ready to strike it rich

Lucky Pierre

We met Pierre Monfette in the lobby of our hotel in Dawson. He is possibly the only person left in the area who digs for gold just as miners did a hundred years ago. During his more than sixteen years of mining, he has struck it rich at least twice on his many claims, but both times he quickly spent all his money. When we met Pierre, he was poor again. He agreed to take us way up into the hills to his mine.

We drove for what seemed hours on the rugged Upper Bonanza Creek Road, past where George Carmack and his partners had made their big find that set off the gold rush.

Finally we reached Pierre's cabin. He had spent a number of winters in the cabin, completely alone but for his dog and a pet mouse.

Pierre's cabin

Pierre showed us his mine shaft, where he'd dug down into the permafrost thirty feet and was mining out below the creek. He had a little generator to run the lights down below. Ernie and I took turns going down the shaft. As in the old days, Pierre did everything by hand. First he thawed the rocky soil until it broke free of the permafrost, and then he drew it up in a bucket. When he got the muck to the surface, he raked it through sieves and then panned it. Pierre showed us some small nuggets he had just panned.

From Pierre's cabin I gazed out over a world of spruce and thought about the stampeders who'd struggled to reach this point, 565 miles from the coast. I thought about the rigors of carrying a ton of equipment and food over the Chilkoot Trail and the White Pass, and all those dead horses along the way. I thought about the few who struck it rich and the thousands who found nothing and gave up.

The worldwide fever that was the gold rush of the Klondike began in 1897 and ended only two years later. But after the stampeders went home, large corporations with machines gained control of the gold fields, and the Klondike has produced gold ever since.

When the Klondike Highway was built in the 1950s, the river, for the most part, returned to the silence of the days before the gold rush. The paddlewheelers stopped running, and the remaining river dwellers moved on.

It was time for us to move on, too. Ernie and I had seen a wild terrain in the stark season that precedes the snows. And we had found the same haunting land that cast its spell on so many dreamers before us.

Special thanks to Ken Coates, the Yukon Archives, Ted and Nicky Harrison, Kim LaPrairie, and Melissa Lourie

Preface verse from "The Spell of the Yukon" by Robert W. Service

Text copyright © 1992 by Peter Lourie
Photographs copyright © 1992 by Peter Lourie
Photographs of northern lights pp. 8 & 35 by Michael Baune. Copyright © 1992 by Michael Baune. Used by permission of the photographer.
Archive photographs courtesy of Yukon Archives at Whitehorse. Used by permission.

Published by Caroline House
Boyds Mills Press, Inc.
A Highlights Company
815 Church Street
Honesdale, Pennsylvania 18431

Publisher Cataloging-in-Publication Data
Lourie, Peter.
        Yukon River : an adventure to the gold fields of the Klondike   / text and photographs by Peter Lourie. --1st ed.
[48] p. : col. ill ; cm.
Summary: An informative text of a canoe trip down the Yukon River; complemented by photographs.
ISBN 1-878093-90-8 hc   •   ISBN 1-56397-878-4 pbk
1. Yukon River--Description and travel. I. Title.
917.98--dc 20   1992
Library of Congress Catalog Card Number: 91-77600

First Boyds Mills Press Paperback Edition, 2000
The text of this book is set in 12-point Stone Serif.
Printed in China

10 9 8 7 6 5 4